Why Republicans Are The Way They Are

Why Republicans Are The Way They Are

by

Frank Barham

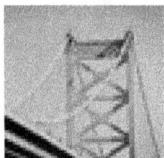

Bridgeview Press
Philadelphia

Greed

Avarice

Selfishness

Shamelessness

Ignorance

Susceptible to Alternate Facts

Republicans are not born. They become. They learn from:

1. family members,
2. community leaders,
3. peers,
4. religious leaders,
5. teachers,
6. Republican politicians,
7. Experiences,
8. the greedy,
9. but mostly from the rich.

Do You, or Someone You Know, Fall into One of the Following Categories of Republicans?

Category 1

Poor-To-Rich

1. These individuals come from a background of poverty where they possessed little in the way of worldly goods, food, clothing, social advantages or status symbols.

2. They felt inferior to others of the same race and were determined to better themselves.

3. They worked two jobs and / or long hours and saved their money, often investing in shoestring endeavors that grew in varying degrees of success but drove their business endeavor / entrepreneurship ever higher up the

financial / social ladder, to a position of independence and varying degrees of high value and wealth.

4. At this juncture, they feel if they can rise above their previously low financial / social status, others can do the same. If others fail, they are simply lazy.

5. They lack empathy or sympathy for those stuck in poverty and often place business interests above employee welfare and safety.[1]

6. They would rather see one hundred individuals (or families) lose their welfare assistance than see one person (or family) with similar, but ill-gotten, assistance at tax payers' expense.

---

[1] https://www.nytimes.com/2016/04/07/us/donald-blankenship-sentenced-to-a-year-in-prison-in-mine-safety-case.html

…But 'tis a common proof
that lowliness is young
ambition's ladder, whereto the
climber upward turns his face.
But when he once attains the
upmost round, he then unto
the ladder turns his back,
looks in the clouds, scorning
the base degrees by which he
did ascend.

Shakespeare
Julius Caesar, Act 2,
Scene 1

Greed is the inventor of injustice as well as the current enforcer.

Julian Casablancas

Man's greed to obtain
something for nothing has
never yet been able to content
itself with a moderate profit.

Will C. Barnes

There is a sufficiency in the world for man's need but not for man's greed.

Mahatma Gandhi

Category 2

Wealth Protectors

1. These people have won, been legally awarded, gifted, inherited, or married into wealth.

2. Asset maintenance is their primary interest. Their secondary interest is asset growth. The less wealthy may see this as selfishness or greed.

3. The concept of personal greed or selfishness is rarely countenanced by Republicans or the wealthy.

4. Asset sharing within a business (401k, stock options, paid pension, etc.) is usually done as a method of stimulating asset growth (in excess of benefit expenses) and not employee welfare.

5. Charitable giving is frequently done to garner social recognition, garner business recognition, garner political standing, or promoting a personal interest—all aimed at reducing the donor's taxes.

6. They believe in small government. This would reduce tax dollars (theirs) necessary to support our government, which is seen as too intrusive, controlling, inept, and restrictive. They believe something short of anarchy would be acceptable.

7. They say they believe private enterprise does a better job of business management than government, which the wealthy controls via lobbyists and political contributions of cash.

8. Items 6 and 7 makes for a greater possibility of reducing business cost, e.g., denying unions, less worksite safety measures, less environmental protection rules that would curtail pollution, and subverts public land use.

I believe in small government
and people taking care of
themselves.

> Susan Olsen
> (Brady Bunch)

Category 3

White Race Protectors

1. These Republicans may be from the poor-to-rich or wealth protector categories.

2. These Republicans are usually Caucasian.

3. They frequently see nonwhite people as inferior to Caucasians.

4. They publicly protest the use of nonwhite workers who are said to be taking jobs that should go to Caucasians.

5. They detest having tax dollars used to support nonwhite persons who need financial assistance for food, clothing, healthcare, etc., because

these people are seen as lazy and unworthy.

6. They prefer Caucasians be the only citizens allowed to vote, because non-Caucasians usually vote Democratic.

7. They prefer fewer tax dollars go to schools in poor neighborhoods because these students and teachers are unworthy.

Category 4

Republicans' Religion

1. Many Republicans claim to be, or pretend to be, religious—many do so for political purposes. Those who appear to be the biggest sinners are the first to say, "My thoughts and **prayers** are with you."

2. Religiously, they believe in "Do as I say" as opposed to do as I do.

3. Most cling to the concept of freedom
of religion but would like to suppress or exclude non-Christian religions.

4. Republicans prefer Old Testament over New Testament concepts. They

tend to ignore the *don'ts* of Deuteronomy (and Romans) except for portions thought to be aimed against the gay community.

5. In keeping with Old Testament beliefs, they often think women are inferior to men who believe women, and a woman's body, should be under the control of men. Unwanted pregnancies are to be endured at all costs, pre and post-delivery.

Wherever men and women are persecuted because of their race, religion, or political views, that place must - at that moment - become the center of the universe.

Elie Wiesel

Category 5

Republican Financial Ideology

1. "I" deserve everything I have.
   (See Category 1 & 2)

2. What is yours should be mine.
   (See Category 2)

3. "I" am willing to use you for my gain.

4. I approve of insider trading if I can avoid litigation.

5. Political power gives "us" the ability to write legislation which allows provides ecological,

financial, banking, and Wall Street privilege for the rich.

6. We hate the outed financial sinner but love the sin.

7. Ill-gotten power gained via any method is sanctioned if there is a chance of non-discovery.

8. All other ideologies are secondary.

As for the Pope, I am too old to be frightened by his shadow and [I] am quite sure his shadow or substance will do less harm to the liberties of my country than will a party, who seeks to acquire political power by exciting religious bigotry in the minds of their duped followers.

Ezra Cornell

The moral angle to the fore-closure crisis, and of course in capitalism, we're not supposed to be concerned with moral stuff, but let's mention it anyway. It shows a culture that is slowly giving in to a futuristic nightmare ideology of computerized greed and unchecked financial violence.

Matt Taibbi

Category 6

Economic Slavery
an
Accepted Republican Belief

Many Republicans see brown, beige, and black skinned people as inferior to white, Anglo-Saxon, people and may be treated as such. This is manifested through:

1. A poor community's educational system is often inferior to systems in rich communities. Republicans have no interest in distributing tax dollars from rich communities school systems to poor school systems.

2. Poorly educated Americans are denied better paying jobs and denied a living wage via low minimum wage legislation.

3. These "inferior" Americans are often denied Medicaid coverage, economic, and other assistance programs.

4. Loss of employment via new technology often leads to employees having no

opportunity for training in other employment situations. Many Republicans believe they, government, or former employers have any responsibility in these areas.

5. Illegal immigrant workers often work in America because employers want to pay as low a wage as possible, e.g., lawn workers, nannies, maids, etc. Many of these workers' economic situation forces them to accept low wages. When these workers are discovered, they are usually deported, but employers rarely face retribution for illegally employing these immigrants.

6. Many Republicans portray economic slaves as a threat to other Americans' employment in low skilled jobs which are dwindling or about to disappear. Where this job reality exists, Republicans use this "economic" threat to mount anti-economic slavery movements for political purposes. To this end, economic slaves are often blamed for job stealing and increasing crimes against Anglo-Saxons.

7. Republicans often refuse to

differentiate between immigrants who seek political / safety asylum verses those who seek to immigrate to America for aspirational purposes.

Category 7

American Oligarchy[2]

Most Republicans' political activities are consciously or unconsciously directed at gaining personal control over others via the mantra of a "smaller" (and more permissive) government and "freedom" to suppress financial ideologies other than their own, e.g., David Koch, Sheldon Adelson.

1. The Supreme Court's 2014 decision to remove limits on corporations' contributions, to political campaign financing reduced the common   man's voice in our democratic government.

2. Large, wealthy corporations can now effectively purchase votes, politicians, judges, and all levels of government.[3]

---

[2] **Merriam-Webster** Dictionary: government by the few The corporation is ruled by *oligarchy*. **2:** a government in which a small group exercises control especially for corrupt and selfish purposes
[3] Please see the movie "Dark Money."

3. Super PACS (political action committees) are groups that can raise and spend unlimited amounts of money to support or oppose a political candidate. The identity of the donors to these groups must be available to the public.

4. 501 (c) (4) groups, contrary to Super PACS, do not have to disclose donor lists and may spend up to 50% of their funds to support or oppress a political entity, i.e., *dark money*. It is possible for foreign actors to donate to these tax-exempt "social" groups. The U.S. government is now looking into possible funneling of Russian money to Trump's election campaign via the NRA.

Republican Ideology
Generalized

1. Gerrymander at every Opportunity

2. It is better to win at all costs than lose by one fault

Republicans' strategy and logistics seem to be aimed at what was stated by the alien race known as the Borg in the movie *Star Wars*.

"You will be assimilated. Resistance is futile."

True Americans will fight back.

Author Information

Frank Barham is a retired physician.

He has seen, first-hand, the deleterious effects of Republicans denying America's poor, its elderly, the ill, and disabled appropriate and sufficient assistance in Republicans' pursuit of selfish financial gains for the wealthy.

He has published several fiction and non-fiction books.

NOTES